Rainbows follow Rain

Books available by Dan Clark:

Forgotten Fundamentals—The Answers Are in the Box
Best or Right—Why Great Is Not Good Enough
The Art of Execution
Chicken Soup for the College Soul
Puppies for Sale and Other Inspirational Tales
Puppies for Sale (Illustrated Storybook)
Clark's Children's Classics
Soul Food, Volumes I and II (Dan's Complete Story Collection)
The Funniest Things Happen When You Look for Laughs
Privilege of the Platform—The Art and Science of Public Speaking
The Thrill of Teaching
The Book of Wisdom, Rhymes, and Wizardry
Lyrical Poetry
Only the Best on Leadership
Only the Best on Customer Service

Rainbows follow Rain

by *New York Times* Best-Selling Author

Dan Clark

CFI
Springville, Utah

ISBN 13: 978-1-59955-039-8

Published by CFI, an imprint of Cedar Fort, Inc., 2373 W. 700 S., Springville, UT, 84663
Distributed by Cedar Fort, Inc. www.cedarfort.com

Cover design by Nicole Williams
Cover design © 2007 by Lyle Mortimer
Edited and typeset by Annaliese B. Cox

Printed in the United States of America

10 9 8 7 6 5 4 3 2 1

Printed on acid-free paper

Acknowledgments

For my special teachers who believed in me when others wouldn't: Ms. Dubois, Mrs. Inman, Dr. Morray, Mrs. Smart, Principal Richards, Mr. Croft, Mr. Thorem, and Coaches Din Morris, Brooks, Allen, Wageman, Trost, Martin, Weight, Simons, Banker, Zimmer, McBride, and Gadd.

For Russ Anderson, Don Pugh, Doug Miller, Fran Peak, Dick Nourse, Zig Ziglar, Jim and Karen Koeninger, Norm Gibbons, Lila Bjorkland, Micky Fisher, Jennifer Lapine, Ernie Wilhoit, Don Wilson, Kay Baker, Pat Mutch, Steve Cosgrove, Les Hewitt, Don Gale, Michael Gale, Chuck Coonradt, Charles Reid, Steve Munn, Wayne and Ruby Clark, Paul Clark, Kelly Clark, Gen. Hal Hornburg (Ret.), Maj. Gen. Johnny Weida, and Laura Calchera (Supreme Commander) for helping me launch my career and/or take it to the next level.

For my National Speakers Association inspiration: Mark Victor Hansen, Jack Canfield, Gail Larsen, Naomi Rhode, Dave Gordon, Robert Henry, Renee Strom, Keith Harrell, Roger Crawford, Bubba Bechtol, Grady Jim Robinson, Jim Tunney, Jeanne Robertson, Bob Murphy, Patricia Fripp, Ray Pelletier, Max Dixon, Mark Sanborn, and Art Berg.

For Bill Kimball, Bob and Paul Mendenhall, Dick Clissold, Bill Gibbs, Jay Jensen, Bob Raybould, Lincoln Hanks, President Royden and Sister Derrick, Phillip Gibson, Mark Tuttle, Gary Mangum, Scott Buie, Mark Monsen, Mont Beardall, Blain Hope, Todd Petersen, Colin and Theresa Dunne, Brendan and Evelyn Gibley, Todd Morgan, Brad Morris, and Brent Bowen for your spirituality, commitment to obedience, faith, and influence in my Christian walk with God.

For K.C., Danny, Nikola, McCall, and Alexandrea for finding wisdom, comfort, laughter, and solace in my speeches, stories, anecdotes, and words. I love you and need you in my life forever.

Perseverance

Two frogs fell in a bowl of cream.
One had an optimistic gleam,
But the other took the gloomy view.
"We'll drown," he cried, and without adieu
He gave a last despairing cry,
Flung up his legs and said good-bye.
Said the other frog with a steady grin,
"I can't get out, but I won't give in!
I'll just swim around till my strength is spent,
Then will I die the more content."
Bravely he swam till it would seem
His struggles began to churn the cream.
On top of the butter at last he stopped,
And out of the bowl he gladly hopped.
What of the moral? It's easily found.
If you can't get out, keep swimming around!

Introduction

Inspiration comes in many ways. When someone has his back up against a wall, how he positively and creatively responds inspires us.

Mr. Ling owned a dry cleaning store that had been in the family for years. Then a developer came along and wanted to push Mr. Ling out of his spot. Mr. Ling did not know how to do anything else for a living. He didn't want to lose his store, and he made it clear to the developer that he was going to stay put.

The conflict escalated as the developer built the shopping mall around Mr. Ling's establishment. To get even, the developer put cleaning shops on both sides of Mr. Ling to drive him out of business. Most would have quit—but not Mr. Ling.

The Ling family hadn't been in business for so many years without learning how to compete and survive. To combat the competition, Mr. Ling made a giant sign and hung it above his front door. As a matter of fact, after he hung the sign, Mr. Ling had more business than ever. What did the sign say? THIS WAY TO MAIN ENTRANCE.

There is always a way to survive. When we rise to the level of our competition, we become better. Like Mr. Ling, you might find life hard, but only those who compete are going to survive, thrive, and succeed.

Inspirational stories strengthen us and teach us some of life's lessons. Some of the lessons found in this book that influence me daily are: (1) We must be willing to pay any price and travel any distance to associate with extraordinary individuals; (2) Pain is a signal to grow, not to suffer—once we learn the lesson the pain is teaching, the pain goes away; (3) Pressure is not something that is naturally there—it's created when you question your ability. When you know what you can do, there is never any question; (4) Crisis does not make or break the man or woman—it just reveals the true character within; (5) It is not enough to say, "I will do my best"—we must do what is necessary to succeed. Because of inspiration like this, we have people in our midst who prove that adversity introduces us to ourselves.

Many people throughout history have achieved greatness. It is one thing to achieve greatness in this life when you are conditioned and trained for it by all the necessary ingredients—good parenting, stable home life, financial security, access to education, proper socialization, and nutrition. But what about those who get dealt a different hand? What about the folks who have to struggle against poverty, neglect, abuse, crime, alienation, and disease? What kind of chance do they have to grab the brass ring? It's difficult enough to succeed when all the elements are aligned correctly. Achieving greatness when huge obstacles befall your path is winning an uphill battle and should be applauded and admired.

At first glance, the people who fill these pages may seem as varied as the professions that define them—entertainer, philosopher, scientist, artist, musician, athlete—but a common thread ties them all together. Each overcame great difficulties to achieve their dreams. This book celebrates the human spirit at its finest moment—that moment when all the other voices are saying, "You can't, you won't," and you tell yourself, "I can, I will!"

James A Abbott

(1967–)

James Abbott was the first baseball player to win the Sullivan Award as the nation's outstanding amateur athlete in 1987. Born without a right hand, Abbott spent hours as a youngster bouncing a ball off a wall to practice fielding as well as throwing. He was the standing quarterback on his high school football team, and he showed enough promise as a pitcher to be drafted by the Toronto Blue Jays shortly after graduation. In the 1988 Olympics, Abbott was the first winning pitcher to bring home the gold to the USA in baseball. Abbott went on to pitch for the California Angels and the New York Yankees.

Louisa May Alcott

(1832–1888)

Louisa May Alcott was born into an extremely poor family and became financially responsible for supporting her family when she was just a young teenager. She suffered from nightmares and hallucinations and felt inadequate at her first attempts at writing. Prompted by her wish to promote women's roles and her hatred for slavery, she volunteered to be a nurse in an army hospital in Washington, DC, as a young adult during the Civil War. During this time, Alcott contracted typhoid fever. This experience provided thematic elements for her future works. Although she is most popular for her children's literature, Alcott explored the themes of self expression and women's rights through her adult fiction works.

Maya Angelou

(1928–)

Maya Angelou is an American author, poet, and entertainer best known for her portrayals of strong African American women. Angelou's parents divorced when she was three, after which time she lived with her grandmother. At age seven, she was raped by her mother's boyfriend. After Angelou testified in court against the man, he was murdered. She did not speak for five years after the man's murder, and she experienced terrible nightmares and feelings of despair and abandonment. In her lifetime, Angelou has worked as a streetcar conductor, dancer, short-order cook, singer, civil rights activist, journalist, poet, editor, and teacher. Much of Angelou's writing stresses the themes of courage, perseverance, self-acceptance, and realization of one's full potential.

Aristotle

(384–322 BC)

Aristotle was one of the most famous of the Greek philosophers. He was a disciple of Plato for nineteen years. He taught in Athens, where hundreds gathered to hear him expound on his theories of metaphysics and ethics—theories that are still studied today. His works included *De Anima*, *Metaphysics*, and *Nicomachean Ethics*. Aristotle stuttered when he spoke!

Lance Armstrong

(1971–)

National and world champion cyclist, two time Olympian, renowned humanitarian, role model, cancer survivor, and six-time winner of the Tour de France, Lance Armstrong is clearly one of the most celebrated and charismatic contributors to the sport of cycling. Armstrong was literally forced off his bike in excruciating pain in October of 1996. Tests revealed advanced testicular cancer that had spread to his lungs and his brain. Chances for his recovery were far less than 50 percent as a frightened but determined Armstrong began an aggressive form of chemotherapy. Remarkably, the chemotherapy began to work, and Armstrong gradually allowed his thoughts to return to racing. He began riding and training only five months after his diagnosis, still uncertain of his future in the sport but profoundly grateful and resolute. Armstrong described his bout with cancer as "a special wake-up call." Within months of his diagnosis, he heeded the call to activism by forming the Lance Armstrong Foundation to inspire and empower other people with cancer.

Louis Armstrong

(1901–1971)

Louis Armstrong was born in a poor section of New Orleans known as The Battlefield. Shortly after Armstrong's birth, his father deserted the family. Armstrong lived in a house with no running water, and by age seven he was singing in the streets to earn money. Despite his poverty-stricken youth, Armstrong discovered that he had a remarkable musical talent and went on to develop a way of playing jazz, as an instrumentalist and vocalist, that had an indelible impact on all musicians to follow. Armstrong originated scat singing, appeared in more than thirty films as a gifted actor, and was one of the first great celebrities of the twentieth century.

Josephine Baker

(1906–1975)

Josephine Baker's father was a professional musician who eventually abandoned the family, forcing them to struggle with extreme poverty. At age eight, Baker quit school to go to work as a maid. Forced to run away from home as a teenager due to her stepfather's abuse, she had two brief marriages at ages thirteen and fifteen. She experienced little success as a dancer in her early career in the U.S., so she moved to France. During an era of French fascination with African and African American culture, she introduced European audiences to dances originated by blacks and became a huge success. She was a member of the French Resistance movement during World War II, actively participated in the U.S. Civil Rights Movement, and later established an orphanage.

Ludwig van Beethoven

(1770–1827)

Born to an alcoholic father and unhappy mother, the young Beethoven was subjected to a brutal training in music at the hands of his father, who hoped the boy would prove to be another prodigy like Mozart. Despite these hardships, Beethoven embraced music and studied for a time with Franz Joseph Haydn. Beethoven lived in poverty, often deprived of basic necessities, and became aware of his advancing deafness by the time he was thirty years old. He contemplated suicide as a result of these conditions but in the end decided to embrace life and went on to compose some of the most beautiful and treasured music the world has ever known.

Larry Bird

(1956–)

Larry Bird's parents divorced when he was sixteen, and his father committed suicide three years later. After dropping out of Indiana University after only six months, he attended Northwood Institute Junior College for a brief time before dropping out there as well. He was married and divorced within six months and, at one of the lowest points in his life, was finally convinced by university officials to give Indiana State University and basketball another try. He was named collegiate player of the year in 1979 and went on to join the Boston Celtics, where he led the team to a first-place finish in their division and was named Rookie of the Year in 1980. Bird is known as one of the greatest all-around performers in basketball's history and was inducted into the Basketball Hall of Fame in 1998.

Lewis Carroll

(1832–1898)

Lewis Carroll was an English mathematician and photographer, but he is most remembered for his work as a novelist. Carroll stammered when he spoke and lectured as a professor of mathematics. Shy and timid, he did not make friends easily. He thought it undignified for a university professor to write children's books and initially did not intend to publish such classics as *Alice's Adventures in Wonderland* and *Through the Looking-Glass.*

George Washington Carver

(1864–1943)

George Washington Carver was born in Missouri of slave parents. His father died at his birth. As a child he was sickly and stammered when he spoke. He was raised in abject poverty and was unable to attend school. He did not learn to read until he was twenty years old. Fueled by a love of learning, he graduated from Iowa State College of Agriculture in 1894. He went on to become an outstanding innovator in the agricultural sciences. He also taught former slaves farming techniques for self-sufficiency. He is most famous for his experiments and subsequent development of industrial uses with peanuts.

Miguel de Cervantes

(1547–1616)

Throughout most of his life, Cervantes struggled financially and was unable to support himself through his writing. He never attained a ranking above private in his career as a soldier, and while serving in the army, he suffered the loss of a hand. When he was twenty-eight years old, he was captured and held as a slave in Algiers for five years. Much of his masterpiece, *Don Quixote*, was written while Cervantes was in prison.

Charlie Chaplin

(1889–1977)

Chaplin was born and raised in the slums of London. His parents separated shortly after he was born. When his mother was no longer able to care for Charlie and his brother, they were admitted to Lambeth Workhouse and, later, Hanwell School for Orphans and Destitute Children. Chaplin's father eventually died of alcoholism, and his mother suffered from mental illness so severe that she often did not recognize her own sons. Chaplin is widely accepted as one of the greatest comedians of the silent era. He was knighted in 1975.

Ray Charles

(1930–2004)

When Charles was five, his four-year-old brother George drowned in an outside tub. Charles witnessed him fall and tried to pull him out, but George was too heavy for him. Not long after this event, Charles began to go blind. He was totally blind by the age of seven. Sources attribute Charles's blindness to glaucoma. He attended school at the Florida School for the Deaf and Blind as a charity case, and he learned how to read Braille there. He also learned how to write music and play various instruments. While he was there, his mother died. His father died two years later. After he left school, Charles began working as a musician in Florida in several bands that played in various styles, including jazz and country music. Ray Charles went on to become a pioneering American pianist and soul musician who shaped the sound of rhythm and blues.

Cesar Chavez

(1927–1993)

Chavez's parents were illiterate migrant farm workers. His family moved to California during the Great Depression. His firsthand experience of the miseries and inequities endured by farmers prompted him to become a union organizer and social activist. He founded the National Farm Workers Association, later known as the United Farm Workers. He led a five-year boycott against California grape growers, protesting poor working conditions and the use of pesticides harmful to farm workers. The boycott became a cause célèbre and was successful in winning new rights for workers.

Anton Chekhov

(1860–1904)

Chekhov suffered beatings and child labor abuses while working in his father's store. His father's cruel temper brought hatred from the family, and Chekhov shouldered the brunt of the abuse. Chekhov was a poor student and failed his graduation exams twice before going on to become one of the most famous Russian dramatists of modern times.

Cher

(1946–)

Cher's drug-addicted and alcoholic father abandoned the family when she was just one year old. Cher was raised by her mother, who was married eight times. She was dyslexic in a time when the condition was not readily detected and had trouble with her schoolwork, eventually dropping out of high school. Cher was sexually molested as a teenager and developed a defiant "bad" attitude. She began living with Sonny Bono at age sixteen. In April of 1965 the duo experienced their fist big hit with the single "Just You." After years of struggling, the couple found success in the 1970s with their hit TV variety show. By 1974 the couple's marriage was coming to an end. Cher went on to have one of the most successful and sustained careers in entertainment history as a singer and critically acclaimed actress.

Frederic Chopin

(1810–1849)

Chopin suffered ill health throughout his short life. He is considered one of the greatest composers of all time, best known for his ballads, etudes, waltzes, and preludes. It was his drive, however, that contributed to his constant illness. He met and fell in love with Maria Wodzinski and was engaged to be married under the condition that he take better care of his health. The engagement was unofficial and did not end in marriage, for after a year-long "trial" period, Maria's parents, disturbed by the bad state of the health of her fiancé—who was seriously ill in the winter—and especially by his irregular lifestyle, viewed him as an unsuitable partner for their daughter. Chopin found this rejection extremely painful, and he died before the age of forty.

Winston Churchill

(1874–1965)

Churchill had few friends growing up and often performed poorly in school. He failed the entrance exams to the Royal Military College three times before he was accepted. His parents were remote and emotionally distant. His father considered Churchill lacking in intelligence and thought the only potential his son had was to be a soldier in the army. Churchill went on to become one of the most famous world leaders history has ever known.

Loretta Claiborne

(1953–)

Loretta Claiborne was the middle of seven children in a poor, single-parent family. Born partially blind and mildly retarded, she was unable to walk or run until the age of four. Eventually, though, she began to run. At first she used her speed and strength to protect herself against cruel classmates, but before she knew it, she had crossed the finish lines of twenty-five marathons, twice placing among the top one hundred women in the Boston Marathon. She has carried the torch in the International Special Olympics, has won medals in dozens of its events, and holds the current women's record in her age group for the 5,000-meter run at seventeen minutes. Claiborne is a celebrated athlete who was honored in 1996 with ESPN's ESPY Arthur Ashe Award for Courage. She credits the Special Olympics with helping her realize that her tremendous athletic talent and role model status could be used to inspire others.

Roberto Walker Clemente

(1934–1972)

Born in Puerto Rico in abject poverty, Roberto Clemente used to practice hitting using tree branches and tin cans. His parents discouraged his desire to play baseball by burning the bat he had carved from a guava tree. Despite their lack of support, he signed with New York's Brooklyn Dodgers and in 1954 joined the Pittsburgh Pirates. After a 1956 automobile accident, Clemente played despite chronic back pain. A host of other serious ailments plagued him during his career, but his performance consistently belied his anguish. He was voted the Most Valuable Player in the National League in 1966, the same year his peers named him Outstanding Player of the Year. Robert Clemente's career ended tragically on December 31, 1972, when he died in a plane crash en route to Nicaragua with supplies for earthquake victims.

Christopher Columbus

(1451–1506)

Columbus was unable to get financial support from the King of Portugal for his voyage. When he eventually received three small ships, the crews were composed of criminals and undesirables. Not all of his voyages to the New World were successful; he endured imprisonment, sickness, mutinies, and exile. He died not knowing he had discovered a New World.

Confucius

(551–479 BC)

Under a corrupt ruler, Confucius was forced to leave his home and wander throughout China for thirty years. He never found support for his teachings or validation for his wisdom during his lifetime. Confucius is one of the most quoted philosophers of all time.

Marie Curie

(1867–1934)

Marie Curie was born in Warsaw at a time when Poland was under Russian domination after the unsuccessful revolt of 1863. She grew up in poverty, losing her mother to tuberculosis at the age of ten. Curie was a diligent worker and spent many years enduring harsh conditions in a cold, dilapidated, leaky shed with primitive and inadequate scientific equipment. She often went without food and sleep for long periods of time. After the 487th experiment had failed, her husband, Pierre, exclaimed, "It will never be done, maybe in a hundred years, but never in our day." The Curies were awarded the Nobel Prize in 1903 for their research on radioactivity. Marie was also awarded the Nobel Prize in 1911 for recognition of her work in discovering radium and polonium.

Salvador Dali

(1904–1989)

Dali's parents named him after his older brother, who died three years before Dali's birth from meningitis, and raised him as their deceased son. Unable to fulfill his parents' irrational expectations, Dali became aggressive and hyperactive. His behavior spiraled into the eccentric and bizarre, and he was expelled from school when he refused to let the teachers grade his art work. Dali joined the Paris Surrealist Group in 1929 and found his niche. He is established as one of the greatest surrealist painters of his time, and his works are displayed in distinguished museums worldwide.

Charles Dickens

(1812–1870)

Dickens's family was considered middle class. However, his father brought the family to financial disaster by his extravagant spending and was imprisoned for debt. Charles was the oldest of the Dickens children and, as a result of his father's imprisonment, was withdrawn from school and sent to work in a factory. During this period, Dickens lived alone and considered this the most terrible time in his life. Nevertheless, it was this experience that shaped and inspired him to pen such masterpieces as *A Tale of Two Cities*, *Great Expectations*, and *David Copperfield*.

Thomas Edison

(1847–1931)

Edison was dyslexic and suffered from a hearing ailment. He was labeled a daydreamer and was removed from school in the first grade, never to return to formal education. He was publicly beaten by his father and began working at age seven. His constant experiments alienated him from his community and he failed more than 10,000 times before he successfully invented the incandescent lightbulb. He once stated, "My father thought I was stupid, and I almost decided I must be a dunce."

Albert Einstein

(1879–1955)

As a child, Einstein was labeled mentally slow and unsociable. His own father was annoyed with his eccentricities. When Einstein first applied to the Zurich Polytechnic Academy, he failed the entrance exams. Despite receiving a teaching certificate in mathematics and physics, he was unable to find a job in Germany because he was Jewish. Einstein was an unknown patent clerk in Bern, Switzerland, when at age twenty-six he published the Theory of Relativity.

Gloria Estefan

(1957–)

Born in Havana, Cuba, Gloria Estefan was raised primarily in Miami after her father, a bodyguard in the employ of Cuban President Batista, was forced to flee the island following the 1959 coup led by Fidel Castro. When Estefan was ten years old, her father was diagnosed with multiple sclerosis, and she cared for him while her mother worked. In 1975, Estefan and her cousin joined the Miami Latin Boys. The band was later christened the Miami Sound Machine and went on to enjoy success with their original fusion of pop, disco, and salsa influences. In 1990, her tour bus was struck by a tractor-trailer. Estefan sustained broken vertebrae in the accident and was not expected to walk again. However, through extensive surgery and the endurance of crippling pain and months of physical therapy, Estefan was back on stage performing in a year.

Galileo

(1564–1642)

Galileo was labeled an absent-minded stargazer by his father. He failed medical school, and his theories and writings were continually in conflict with the religious beliefs of his day. He was forbidden by the Inquisition to publish his books and articles, so he wrote his third and final book secretly from prison. He went blind while imprisoned and never even saw the printed copy. He said of this book, "I esteem this the most of all my works. It is the outcome of my extreme agony."

Marvin Gaye

(1939–1984)

Marvin Gaye was the second of three children born to Marvin Sr., a minister in the House of God (a conservative Christian sect that fuses elements of Judaism and Pentecostalism, imposes strict codes of conduct, and observes no holidays). Gaye began singing in the choir at the age of three. Later he took up the drums and piano. He used music to escape from the nightmarish reality of his home life; throughout his childhood, his father beat him severely on an almost daily basis. He started working as a Motown session drummer and playing on early hits by Smokey Robinson and the Miracles. Upon embarking on a solo career, Gaye struggled to find his voice, and early singles failed. But he persevered and soon was charting hit after hit. His music evolved into social commentary on the sweeping changes occurring during the late sixties, and he was prolific in his musical career until his life was ended on April 1, 1984, when his father fatally shot him after a heated argument.

Ulysses S Grant

(1822–1885)

Ulysses S. Grant was the American commander of the Union Forces during the Civil War and the eighteenth president of the United States. However, his early career was less than stellar. At age thirty-two, he was forced to resign from the army as a result of his chronic alcoholism. He tried his hand at farming and real estate and, after failing at both attempts, returned to his father's tanning shop for the only work he could find. At age thirty-nine, he was given the command of a volunteer regiment in Illinois. Seven years later, he became the president of the United States.

Nathaniel Hawthorne

(1804–1864)

As a child, Hawthorne was shy and aloof. He was emotionally deprived and neglected and suffered a crippling accident while still a young boy. Most of his childhood was spent alone. As an adult, Hawthorne secured work in a customs house, but he hated his job and felt he was a failure because he couldn't support his family through his true passion—writing. He was eventually fired from his job, and while writing *The Scarlet Letter,* he became sick and terribly depressed. Hawthorne was eventually recognized as one of the greatest writers of the nineteenth century.

Audrey Hepburn

(1929–1993)

While the Hepburns were vacationing at their home in Holland, Hitler's army took over the town where they were staying. Hepburn watched as friends and neighbors were forced at gunpoint onto trucks that would deliver them to the camps. Hepburn made a daring escape and was forced to hide in a rat-infested cellar for several weeks. As a result of the trauma, she suffered from malnutrition and was plagued with anorexia for the rest of her life. She began her career as a model but was soon discovered by a producer, and her acting career was born. Hepburn received an Academy Award for Best Actress for her role in Roman Holiday. She traveled extensively in her later years as a goodwill ambassador for the United Nations Children's Fund, helping thousands of underprivileged children throughout the world.

Billie Holiday

(1915–1959)

Billie Holiday's grandfather was one of seventeen children born of a black Virginia slave and a white Irish plantation owner. Holiday's mother was only thirteen when Billie was born. Holiday first heard the music of Louis Armstrong and Bessie Smith at Alice Dean's, the Baltimore house of ill repute where she ran errands and scrubbed floors as a young girl. She made her singing debut in obscure Harlem nightclubs, then toured with Count Basie and Artie Shaw before embarking on a solo career. Despite a lack of technical training and extreme racial and gender discrimination inherent in the music business at the time, Holiday's unique diction, inimitable phrasing, and acute dramatic intensity made her the outstanding jazz singer of her day.

Steven Jobs

(1955–)

Considered an odd child, Steven Jobs burned his hand badly after introducing a hairpin to an electrical socket. He had trouble in school and was suspended at age nine for defiantly refusing to complete his work. Jobs had trouble making friends and was considered different by the other children and his teachers. He dropped out of college and experimented with drugs. During his first job at Atari, he worked alone at night because he refused to bathe on a regular basis. When Jobs was twenty-one years old, he and Stephen Wozniak created the Apple I computer in Jobs's bedroom. He was named Entrepreneur of the Decade in 1989 by *Inc.* magazine.

James Earl Jones

(1931–)

Jones was abandoned by his father and only saw his mother occasionally; thus, he was raised by his grandparents. He developed a stuttering problem that was so severe that for years he spoke only when necessary and often could only communicate through written word. He later took up acting to combat his condition and earned his bachelor's degree in drama from the University of Michigan. Soon he was performing on Broadway and enjoying a successful acting career in film and television. Considering his early struggles with speaking, it is wonderfully ironic that Jones is best known for his powerful voice-over work as Darth Vader in *Star Wars*, King Mufasa in *The Lion King*, and, most recently, the "voice" of CNN.

Frida Kahlo

(1907–1954)

Frida Kahlo was stricken with polio at age six, which left her right leg much thinner than her left. At age eighteen, she was involved in a serious bus accident that left her with a broken spinal column, collarbone, ribs, and pelvis and eleven fractures in her right leg. In addition, her right foot was crushed and her shoulder was dislocated. For a month, Kahlo was forced to stay flat on her back, encased in a plaster cast and enclosed in a boxlike structure. Kahlo's extraordinary will to live helped her make a remarkable recovery. She started painting shortly after the accident as she was bored in bed. It became her lifelong passion. Although Kahlo's recovery was nothing short of miraculous, she suffered painful relapses and was plagued by fatigue for the rest of her life. Kahlo married Diego Riveras, the famous muralist, in 1929. Although their marriage was tempestuous, they were supportive of each other's work and talent.

John Keats

(1795–1821)

The English poet, best known for his work *Ode on a Grecian Urn*, was the son of a stable keeper. As a result of living in exposed conditions, he developed tuberculosis. Keats studied medicine but gave up this pursuit to write poetry. Although he is one of the most studied and revered poets in English literature, his works were often met with harsh criticism during his lifetime. He died at the young age of twenty-six.

Helen Keller

(1880–1968)

Keller became blind and deaf after an illness before she was two years old. Through the stubborn dedication of her teacher, Anne Sullivan, Keller was able to emerge from her dark and silent world to become an author and social activist. She achieved distinction as a lecturer and scholar, mastered many languages, and received a degree from Radcliffe College.

Martin Luther King Jr.

(1929–1968)

Martin Luther King Jr. is one of the most influential and important figures in American history. A clergyman and civil rights leader, he was the youngest person ever to receive the Nobel Prize. As a boy, he rebelled against religion and was planning a future as a doctor before he joined the ministry. He endured abuse from critics and former friends in his struggle for non-violent change in the treatment of African Americans. At thirty-eight, he had been jailed nineteen times; he once stated, "I will rot in jail before I make a butchery of my conscience."

John Lennon

(1940–1980)

Lennon's parents divorced when he was four. When his mother became neglectful, he was sent to live with his aunt and uncle. He later lost his uncle when he was fifteen years old and hid his unhappiness through drinking and rebellious behavior. He enjoyed a brief reunion with his mother, only to lose her once more when she was hit by a car and killed. Lennon was devastated. He was quoted once as saying, "I was different all my life . . . nobody seems to understand where I'm coming from." Lennon formed The Quarrymen in 1958 and focused his energy into music. It was the perfect outlet for his creative imagination. He was then introduced to Paul McCartney, George Harrison, and Ringo Starr. John, Paul, George, and Ringo soon became The Beatles, one of the most successful rock groups of all time.

Loretta Lynn

(1935–)

Loretta Lynn was a coal miner's daughter and the second of eight children. She was raised in abject poverty in a small shack during the Great Depression. She was married by the time she was thirteen, had four children and several miscarriages by age eighteen, eventually had two more children, and became a grandmother by age twenty-nine. Her husband encouraged her singing talent and helped get her recognized by Don Grashey of Zero Records, who took her to Los Angeles in 1960, where she recorded four of her own songs. Zero had no money for promotion, so Lynn and her husband, Mooney, promoted her song, "I'm A Honky Tonk Girl" themselves. Mooney said they "drove 80,000 miles to sell 50,000 copies," but the song reached number fourteen on the country charts, and Lynn was on her way to becoming one of the best-loved country singers in the nation.

Ferdinand Magellan

(1480–1521)

The Portuguese explorer organized the first expedition to go around the world. Not only did he have to combat the common belief at the time that the world was flat, but he also endured severe storms, mutiny, and sickness. On the voyage that proved to the world that the earth is indeed round, he subsisted on a diet of rats and leather.

Isaac Newton

(1642–1727)

As a child, Newton was described as unruly and temperamental with unpredictable behavior. He was born prematurely and was not expected to live. Although he survived, he was often sick as a child. Many of Newton's greatest discoveries were made during the time of the Plague, when he was forced to work at home after the closure of Cambridge University. Newton went on to discover the laws of gravity and motion.

Eleanor Roosevelt

(1884–1962)

Eleanor Roosevelt's grandmother was a strict disciplinarian who was in charge of raising her after Roosevelt's mother died of diphtheria when she was just eight years old. Her father was an alcoholic with suicidal tendencies and died just two years later. While her mother was still alive, she would ridicule Roosevelt for her lack of beauty and showed her no affection. As a result, Roosevelt was shy and very awkward, writing stories about lonely children who longed for love. Later she would grow up to be First Lady and one of the most influential women of her time. She was a proponent for social causes and was a passionate advocate for the weak and disadvantaged.

Wilma Rudolph

(1940–1994)

Wilma Rudolph suffered from double pneumonia, followed by scarlet fever and polio, during her childhood. Her left leg was paralyzed, so she could not walk or run. She wore metal braces on her legs until she was eleven. Rudolph went on to become one of the finest track and field athletes the sport has ever seen. She was the first female athlete to win three gold medals in a single Olympics (Rome 1960): 100-meter, 200-meter, and 400-meter relay. Described as one of the greatest sprinters of all time, she was inducted into the Women's Sports Hall of Fame in 1980 and the National Women's Hall of Fame in 1994. She died tragically of brain cancer in 1994 in her home in Nashville, Tennessee. She said, "I never forget all the years when I was a little girl and not able to be involved. When I ran, I felt like a butterfly."

Jonas Salk

(1914–1995)

Despite opposition, intense scrutiny, skepticism, public fears, and bad press, Jonas Salk never wavered in his research and development of a vaccine for polio. He worked eighteen-hour days and suffered countless failed attempts. Dedicated to finding a cure, he was resolute in his work and developed the first vaccine against polio in 1952. Mass immunizations were instituted and countless lives saved as a result of Salk's unwavering commitment to putting an end to this dreaded disease.

Barbra Streisand

(1942–)

Barbra Streisand's father died before she was two years old, leaving her mother emotionally devastated and incapable of caring for her. She moved from one relative to the next before her mother remarried when Streisand was eight. She endured a terrible relationship with her stepfather, who constantly criticized her and was abusive to her mother. Streisand was often the victim of cruel taunting and was labeled *mieskeit*, which is Yiddish for "ugly person." Her stepfather left when Streisand was fourteen, and she blamed herself for the break-up. She began her singing career in New York nightclubs and finally made a breakthrough with a part in the Broadway show *I Can Get It for You Wholesale*. Streisand released albums and performed nonstop until she became a bona fide singing star. She then went on to acting, starring in many comedic roles as well as her unforgettable performance in *The Way We Were*. She garnered critical acclaim for her work as a director for *Yentl* and *Prince of Tides*. Streisand took a twenty-year break from performing live concerts before she returned to the stage in 1994 for one of the most highly anticipated comeback concerts in musical history.

Harry S. Truman

(1884–1972)

The thirty-second president of the United States never went to college. After being denied entrance to West Point because of his poor eyesight, he went into the men's clothing business, only to have that venture fail three years later. After trying his hand at a number of other occupations, he entered political life, where he never thought he would advance beyond the Senate. As president during the end of World War II, Truman was responsible for making some of the most important and difficult decisions of our time.

Tina Turner

(1939–)

Tina Turner is the triumphant survivor of a very difficult childhood and an abusive marriage to Ike Turner. After her parents moved to the city, Turner was raised by her paternal grandmother. Turner was finally reunited with her mother and sister at age sixteen. In 1960 she joined Ike Turner's band. The duo's track record in the sixties and seventies is the stuff of legend, as is the violent disintegration of their marriage and Tina's subsequent departure. For a time, Turner struggled for survival, depending on food stamps and the kindness of friends. In 1984, she made one of the biggest comebacks in music history with the release of her solo album *Private Dancer*. Turner has been inducted into the Rock 'n' Roll Hall of Fame and has received a star on the Hollywood Walk of Fame.

AMAZING KIDS

Heartsongs

Mattie Stepanek was born with Dysautonomic Mitochondrial Myopathy, a condition that interrupts autonomic, or automatic, functioning such as breathing, heart rate, blood pressure, body temperature, digestion, and utilization of oxygen. This rare form of muscular dystrophy had already claimed the lives of his three older siblings. Mattie passed away from the debilitating disease just shy of his fourteenth birthday. What could have been the most tragic story a child could tell in his own short life, Mattie turned into a tale of heroic courage and poetic inspiration.

Mattie liked to speak about peace efforts and global tolerance. He spoke to school children and business leaders, medical personnel and church groups, firefighters and Harley Davidson riders, all across America. Mattie loved talking to anyone who loved to listen. One of his favorite speeches was when he got to introduce his hero, former president Jimmy Carter, at the Kennedy Center in Washington, DC.

Mattie shared his messages of hope and peace on many television programs. He appeared on *The Oprah Winfrey Show*; *Larry King Live*; *Good Morning, America*; *Primetime*; *The Today Show*; and many other programs on several different occasions. He also helped with the Jerry Lewis Labor Day Telethon. In 2002, he drove cross country with his mom and friends to be in Los Angeles for the telethon. He loved getting to see his country coast to coast.

Instead of feeling cheated, Mattie felt truly blessed and very lucky to have met so many wonderful people during his journey through life. He became friends with lots of great people, including Jimmy Carter, Oprah Winfrey, Larry King, Christopher Cross, Lance Bass, and Billy Gilman.

Mattie wrote poetry that was both breathtakingly beautiful and unbelievably accomplished for someone so young. He inspired thousands through his verse, and in 2003, Mattie and Billy Gilman collaborated on a CD project, *Music through Heartsongs*. On the CD, Billy sings twelve of Mattie's favorite poems, which were set to various styles of music, including Celtic, soft rock, Hawaiian, country, jazz, and pop-Christian style. One of his favorite tracks, "I AM/Shades of Life," was made into a music video, in which Mattie made a cameo appearance.

Children born with his disease do not usually live very long. Mattie knew that each day was a gift, and he made the most of it. He said he got his strength from God and his mom, and also from the people that became part of his circle of life. "People tell me I inspire them. And that inspires me. It's a beautiful circle, and we all go around together, with and for each other. What a gift."

One Play at a Time

At a time when science still falls short of understanding hereditary disabilities, it also faces a challenge in transforming them into a source of motivation for creativity and innovation. History is full of heroes who overcame their handicaps and were distinctive among their peers in literature, music, and other academic or leadership positions. The students of Ideal Education School in Kuwait are no different in their perseverance and strong will to excel, despite their different physical challenges.

Twenty-four students turned their vision into reality as they stood before an audience to present the musical play "Life Is a Celebration," thereby defying all the odds that could hamper their brighter view of life, through music and dance and a refusal to let their physical conditions become limitations.

The play's producer, school teacher Dawn Jawhar, said the play is just one way through which these children fight back against their predicaments. After extensive training and long hours of rehearsals, the children presented the musical play emphasizing the joy of life and willpower. The play comprises songs, dances, and theatrical musical roles that shed light on the challenges of those with special needs and, at the same time, combines art and inspiration to leave audiences not only impressed by the accomplishments of these special kids but determined, perhaps, to overcome their own obstacles with grace and a renewed commitment to excellence.

Down But Not Out

Practically all of Timothy Legere's life has been about defying expectations. A foster child since he was thirteen months old, Legere is a smart, well-adjusted, college-bound, straight-A student who says his life holds a lesson not only for other youths like him but also for adults who write off foster children and their chances of success.

There are stereotypes about kids in the foster-care system: they'll never make it to college, they're not smart, they'll never succeed, and they'll most likely end up in jail. But Timothy Legere is a shining example of how untrue that stereotype can be. Legere, along with 150 other foster youths, stepped proudly onto the stage of the Walt Disney Concert Hall to be recognized for their academic achievement in a ceremony that marked not only their graduation from high school, but their transition to new, independent, and successful lives.

The students, who will attend colleges, universities, and vocational schools across the nation, received more than $675,000 in scholarships, as well as stipends to purchase business attire for interviews.

Every one of these kids has seen things most kids shouldn't have to see, and they have had to overcome obstacles that most kids shouldn't even have to think about. Nationally each year, about twenty thousand teens "age out" of the foster care system when they turn eighteen. Although slightly more than half of those youths earn a high school diploma, only about 5 percent attend college and more than 25 percent end up homeless after exiting the system, according to the U.S. Census and other government data. About 30 percent of such youths suffer severe emotional, behavioral, or developmental problems.

The message from Legere and others like him is one of resilience and the belief that anything is possible. If you dream it, you can do it.

Ride 'Em Cow-boy

High School sophomore Billy Brower has always wanted to be a cowboy, and thanks to a horse named Garth, his boyhood dream has come true. Billy and twenty-one other families were invited to attend a unique, week-long camp designed especially for handicapped children. These families were guests of the Whitney Hope Foundation, a not-for-profit organization funded solely by the generous donations of caring individuals, churches, and corporations. Together, they share the belief with founder Dan Whitney that handicapped children can advance from the sidelines and be active participants in the full camping experience, just like other boys and girls who attend traditional summer camps.

Dean and his wife, Kim Brower, are no strangers to camping. They have involved their son and daughter in family outings since infancy and continued camping with them even after both children became disabled. Billy sustained a massive stroke when he was four and a half months old, leaving him dependant on his parents for his basic needs, even to this day. As a result of the stroke, he has a disease known as Cerebral Palsy. He is confined to a wheelchair and needs assistance being transferred to and from his chair.

His older sister, Lindsey, became disabled when she was nine and a half years old. She suffered over 125 strokes, followed by a massive stroke that placed her in a coma for four months. Lindsey, unlike her brother, is not in a wheelchair. However, she has partial hearing loss, uses a cane for balance, and is legally blind. Both Lindsey and Billy have learned not to let their disabilities prevent them from participating in normal teenage activities. They are involved in Girl Scouts and Boy Scouts, and their parents are the troop leaders. Dean and Kim have masterminded numerous summer scout camps, as well as day camps, but have always felt their children were left out because of their limitations and disabilities. Not so with Camp Whitney Hope!

Dennis and Pam Dutton brought Garth, their beautiful brown horse, to the summer camp for the families to enjoy. Billy had told his parents he wanted to meet Garth, but when he came face to face with the huge beast, Billy suddenly changed his mind. Billy was afraid and screamed as though his life were in danger, while Garth casually sauntered over to greet him, hoping to receive a carrot and at best to meet a new friend.

Kim told her terrified son, "I know you're scared to death, but you're going to touch him." She also knew how badly he wanted to pet Garth since that was all he had talked about for the entire day, saying, "Go see the horse, go touch Garth." His parents are very cautious with Billy's safety, yet they offer him strict encouragement to help him overcome his fears. Their intuition paid off, much to Billy's eventual pleasure.

As Garth cautiously nuzzled close to his new friend, Billy reached up, petted him on his side, and gave him several carrots. The bond between Billy and Garth grew throughout the remainder of the week at camp, with Billy going to visit him each day. This special bond between a young handicapped teenage boy and a horse continued after the conclusion of camp. Billy is now grooming, feeding, and riding Garth at a horse ranch in Santa Paula, California. He began by sitting in a saddle accompanied either by Pam Dutton or her son, Dean, who would sit behind Billy while he held onto the horn of the saddle. Garth was led by one of his owners while both Dean and Kim Brower walked on each side of the horse, giving their son words of praise and encouragement as he swayed back and forth to the movement of his faithful friend.

The horseback rides have helped strengthen his back and relax his muscles. His parents have said that Billy's physical therapist noticed an improvement in his muscle tone. Going to the horse ranch has also improved his speech development and broadened his vocabulary.

The Boy Scouts of America certified Pam Dutton as an instructor in horsemanship, and Billy is earning this badge. Because of a special saddle Pam and her husband Dennis constructed to support his back, Billy rode solo for the first time. He held on tight and sat up as straight as possible, riding high in the saddle and beaming from ear to ear. On this crisp autumn day as the sun began to set, Billy became the true cowboy he once only dreamed of becoming!

Billy now proclaims, "No fear of the horse. I rode the horse by myself." All because he was given an opportunity to fulfill a dream, both of riding a horse and going to a camp where he was treated just like other kids who are like him.

Note: Garth, a fifteen-hundred-pound horse that was destined for disposal three years ago, is a prime example of the hope and proof that we all have a purpose to fulfill.

New Memories

Dana Kiger's "situation" began March 5, 2005, when she hit her heard during a soccer game fall. She sustained a brain injury that led to a rare form of amnesia. For the first few days after her fall, Dana didn't know who she was or what had happened to her—that became shockingly apparent when she awoke at the hospital and didn't know her mom and dad or her brother and sister. Two years later, Dana still can't remember her childhood or early teen years. But she has rebuilt her life. People have asked her thousands of times, "Don't you want your memory back?" Her response to that question is, "I really don't want to go back. I'd rather go forward."

Dana didn't start going forward for five months, until doctors gave her the clearance to resume playing soccer. She wore headgear for half of the season, but her parents still winced when she hit the ball with her head. "I was not scared at all. I didn't remember the pain I was in when I hit my head. I didn't want this to stop me from living my life," she said.

Eventually, her soccer skills returned, as did her stamina. A constant throughout the recovery process was her mental toughness. Those traits earned her the Ohio High School Athletic Association's Most Courageous Athlete Award in the spring of 2006 and led Slippery Rock University coaches to offer Dana a soccer scholarship.

"She is a true inspiration to us all," head coach Noreen Herlihy said. "Hers is an amazing story of courage. We look forward to having her join our program."

It's only fitting that Dana plans to major in one of SRU's specialized fields of study, physical therapy, so she can help others recover. "Amnesia has made me stronger. Knowing that you're just one play away from losing it all, knowing that you can't remember anything, makes you want to work real hard for the things you do remember."

The Price of a Miracle

Tess was a precocious eight year old when she heard her mom and dad talking about her little brother, Andrew. All she knew was that he was very sick and they were completely out of money. They were moving to an apartment complex next month because her dad didn't have the money for the doctor bills and the house. Only a very costly surgery could save him now, and it was looking like there was no one to loan them the money. She heard her dad say to her tearful mother with whispered desperation, "Only a miracle can save him now."

Tess went to her bedroom and pulled a glass jelly jar from its hiding place in the closet. She poured all the change out on the floor and counted it carefully. Three times, even. The total had to be exactly perfect. No chance here for mistakes. Carefully placing the coins back in the jar and twisting on the cap, she slipped out the back door and made her way six blocks to the drug store. She waited patiently for the pharmacist to give her some attention, but he was too busy talking to someone. Tess twisted her feet to make a scuffing noise. Nothing. She cleared her throat as loudly as she could muster. No good. Finally she took a quarter from her jar and banged it on the glass counter. That did it! "And what do you want?" the pharmacist asked in an annoyed tone of voice. "I'm talking to my brother from Chicago whom I haven't seen in ages," he said without waiting for a reply to his question.

"Well, I want to talk to you about *my* brother" Tess answered back in the same annoyed tone. "He's really, really sick . . . and I want to buy a miracle."

"I beg your pardon?" replied the pharmacist.

"His name is Andrew and he has something bad growing inside his head and my Daddy says only a miracle can save him now. So how much does a miracle cost?"

"We don't sell miracles here, little girl. I'm sorry, but I can't help you," the pharmacist said, softening a little.

"Listen, I have the money to pay for it. If it isn't enough, I will get the rest. Just tell me how much it costs."

The pharmacist's brother was a well dressed man. He stooped down and asked the little girl, "What kind of a miracle does your brother need?"

"I don't know," Tess replied with her eyes welling up. "I just know he's really sick and Mommy says he needs an operation. But my daddy can't pay for it, so I want to use my money."

"How much do you have?" asked the man from Chicago.

"One dollar and eleven cents," Tess answered barely audible. "And it's all the money I have, but I can get some more if I need to."

"Well, what a coincidence," smiled the man. "A dollar and eleven cents—the exact price of a miracle for little brothers." He took her money in one hand, and with the other hand he grasped her mitten and said, "Take me to where you live. I want to see your brother and meet your parents. Let's see if I have the kind of miracle you need."

That well dressed man was Dr. Carlton Armstrong, a surgeon specializing in neurosurgery. The operation was completed without charge, and it wasn't long until Andrew was home again and doing well. Tess's mom and dad were happily talking about the chain of events that had led them to this place.

"That surgery," her mom whispered, "was a real miracle. I wonder how much it would have cost?"

Tess smiled. She knew exactly how much a miracle cost: one dollar and eleven cents . . . plus the faith of a little child. A miracle is not the suspension of natural law but the operation of a higher one.

A Reason to Succeed

In one of Bernard Anthony's earliest memories, his mother had vanished on a drug binge, leaving him alone to care for his two baby sisters. He was two years old. Anthony was lucky. He was rescued and raised by a woman who had no reason to do so other than compassion in her heart. And he wasn't the only one. Seventeen children found their way into Emma Gantt's home on Palo Alto's Wilkie Way. Many were family members, but others were children seeking refuge from horrific situations.

When Anthony, a senior football and basketball player at Gunn High, learned he won San Jose Sports Authority's $2,500 REACH scholarship for overcoming adversity by participating in sports, he knew it wasn't just for him. It was for all of them. In Emma's house, everything the individual does is a reflection of the family. Words like "adoptive" are useless. Nothing distinguishes one over another, regardless of baggage or background. You walked in that door and you were accepted. When you came to that house, you were family. It was no surprise that when a relative called Emma with a story of five siblings suffering from abuse and neglect in his East Oakland neighborhood she came to the rescue.

"There were days when we didn't eat that much, or eat at all," Anthony recalled. Their living conditions were filthy. Their mother was a crack addict and often gone. They lived alternately either in a car or a grandmother's apartment. Emma's nephew, Herbert Price, began feeding the children regularly and asked Emma to bring them home. She did so for days at a time. Meanwhile, she tried to locate the father by advertising in the newspaper and asking around the neighborhood. She had a name—Bernard Anthony Sr.—but nothing else. She never found him. Finally, Child Protective Services officials stepped in. They were prepared to place the children in foster care, but they knew Emma had been looking after the kids and urged her to take custody as an official guardian. She did, and when she went to their home to take the kids, their mother was gone. Emma told the kids to get in the car and lock the doors. They didn't protest. And she sped off.

Anthony found Emma to be caring yet strict. She was an uneducated woman, but she knew life better than any and lived every day by the golden rule. Anthony was taught respect for himself and others, and there was a time in which he struggled with both disciplines.

He was diagnosed with Attention Deficit Hyperactivity Disorder in elementary school and found it difficult to concentrate in class. One teacher called him stupid. "I was easily distracted and extremely hyper," Anthony said. "For a long time, I couldn't cope with it." Then he found salvation in sports. "If I could show how good I was in sports, and play like everybody else, I could be normal," he said. "And if I could be normal on the court, I could be normal in the classroom." With steadfast persistence, Anthony remained in regular classes, holding his own in a high-pressure academic environment. Anthony, a five-foot-ten-inch guard, was defensive player of the year on a playoff team that finished 20-9. When asked if he is grateful for his second chance, Anthony answers, "Very much. That's why I try so hard."

Undefeated

When Shawn was four years old, he was suffering from increasing lethargy, deteriorating eyesight, and severe headaches that were beyond what his body could endure. After several months of seeing an ophthalmologist, his headaches became so intense they were causing him to vomit from the pain. On October 13, 1998, a visit to a local walk-in clinic led to a CAT scan, which revealed his parents' worst fear: he had what appeared to be an abnormality in his brain. An MRI confirmed the presence of a large brain tumor in the middle of his head. The tumor had been blocking off the circulation of the brain fluid, resulting in excessive pressure on the brain, which was the cause of his excruciating headaches. The tumor was also the cause of his loss of eyesight, as it was located in the optic chiasm, where the signal from the eyes to the brain passes through.

Shawn had his first surgery to insert a shunt in his skull to relieve the pressure on his brain. The shunt was successful, but the pressure was so extreme, another shunt had to be inserted shortly after. What an amazing change in Shawn's personality came about in those first few days—he had been in so much pain from the pressure on his brain that it was the cause of his lethargy. His headaches were gone and a new, energized child emerged. A few weeks passed to allow Shawn to heal before starting a long regiment of chemo that lasted thirteen months. The chemotherapy left Shawn nearly bald and physically and mentally exhausted.

On the thirteenth month of his treatment, the doctors told his parents they felt the tumor was under control; if the next MRI showed no additional growth, he would be finished with his treatment. A few days before Christmas, Shawn had his last treatment. The doctors called the day before Christmas with the MRI report and gave them the best Christmas gift ever: Shawn was done with chemo. Routine MRIs would be required in the future to monitor the tumor, but it was under control.

In the winter of 1999, Shawn began wrestling, a very demanding sport but also one sport that Shawn could do even with his loss of vision. Although he was one of only a few kids in the state that wrestled with a handicap, let alone a brain tumor and shunts, he soon became an inspiration and showed people that a huge heart and dedication could overcome anything. In 2002 he finished second in the state, and, hungry for more, in 2004, his fourth year of wrestling, he won his first USA Freestyle State Championship.

Three days after Shawn won the championship, he severely broke his arm in two places while preparing for another huge tournament. When the medics asked Shawn how he was doing, obviously in pain but without a tear in his eye, he said, "I'm fine; it's not like it's brain surgery. I'll be back tomorrow." After months of healing, Shawn came back with a vengeance in 2005, winning the gold medal in his first tournament back from his injury. Even more amazing was that he followed his 2004 championship with a second consecutive state championship in 2005. At only eleven years old, Shawn was undefeated in the 2005/2006 season and on track to win his third USA Washington State Wrestling Championship, which would result in his induction into the Legends of Washington Wrestling.

Walking on Sunshine

Kids often ask Scout Bassett if she wishes she had two normal legs. Bassett answers, "No. I have never known anything different, and it would seem weird to me. Besides, if it weren't for the missing leg, I wouldn't have the opportunities I have today!" What she means is she has learned important lessons about overcoming big challenges to reach her goals. "When you are missing a leg, it teaches you to appreciate little things—like being able to walk and run," she says.

Scout has faced big challenges. Born in China, she was left at an orphanage before her first birthday, suffering from terrible burns. Her right leg was especially damaged, and doctors amputated it above the knee. She remembers being hungry all the time at the orphanage. As soon as she was old enough to get around, she was put to work mopping floors, feeding babies, and washing dishes. And she had to do all that with an artificial leg that didn't work very well. "It was made of things you'd find in your garage," she recalls. "Belt straps, masking tape, nuts and bolts. It didn't feel very good, and clanked, and even fell off sometimes."

Then, when she was seven years old, a family in Michigan adopted her. Everything about her new life in the United States was better, including the improved artificial legs her new parents got for her. First she got a better leg for everyday activities. It was okay for some things, but she still couldn't play soccer or basketball. When she was fourteen, she got a high-tech leg made for sports and put it to the test right away in a race for disabled athletes. "I remember being terrified because this was my first time," she says. "But my doctor said, 'You have to start somewhere.' "

Scout was waiting nervously for the race to start when athlete Sarah Reinertsen came up and said, "I've been doing this for a while. Let me give you some tips." Reinertsen, who lost her leg when she was seven, is the first woman amputee to finish the Ironman triathlon in Hawaii. In the 2005 race, she swam 2.4 miles (3.9 kilometers) in the ocean, biked 112 miles (180 kilometers), and ran 26 miles (42 kilometers). She works with an organization called the Challenged Athletes Foundation to help support people like Scout. Reinertsen's encouragement changed the teenager's life. She lost that first race but gained the confidence that she needed to compete. If Sarah could do it, she could too.

Training hard, she improved her strength and skill step by step. She even took up golf and tennis, and by high school she'd gotten good enough to be on the varsity teams. Now living in California, Scout runs competitively and also finds time to share her story with school groups. "There are days when I study until one in the morning and get up at five to swim and train, and it is tough," she explains. But she has a motto that keeps her going: "The task ahead of you is never greater than the strength inside you."

"Sometimes people look at someone like me or at Sarah and think they have nothing in common with us. I tell them that even if you aren't physically challenged, everybody has challenges of some kind—maybe with family, or homework, or friends. No matter what it is, you can overcome that obstacle," she says. "Everything you need is inside your heart. Take small steps. As time goes by, the steps will get bigger, and you will reach your dream."

You Can't Quit—It's a League Rule

In Dan Clark's humorous, self-deprecating way, he says that when he was born he was so ugly that after he popped out and the doctor slapped him, the doctor then went out into the hall and slapped his dad! For nearly his entire life, Dan has had to deal with adversity and has had to get back up and go again.

Dan battled a cancerous throat abscess at eight years old that had him in the hospital for weeks and almost destroyed his vocal chords. Dan was hit in the face at age twelve with a baseball pitch that resulted in root canals in his front teeth; has broken his neck, nose, and jaw; had his head sewn up eleven times; and has had two hernias. Dan has broken both hands, thumbs, and little fingers, his left wrist, and his right arm; blown out patella tendons in both knees; torn cartilage repaired in seven surgeries on both knees; and broken his right shoulder, requiring a three-inch titanium screw.

When Dan finally got it all together and became the biggest, fastest, and strongest he had ever been, he suffered an injury in football practice that caused his right eye to droop, his speech to slur, his right side to be paralyzed, and his arm to dangle at his side. Fifteen doctors said he would not recover, but after a year of therapy, he did! At almost full strength—wouldn't you know it?—Dan's appendix burst, requiring emergency surgery.

Dan Clark is an expert eyewitness to the facts: no matter what our past has been, we have a spotless future; pain is a signal to grow, not to suffer. Once we learn the lesson the pain is teaching us, the pain goes away; failure is an event, not a person; if we're not failing a few times, it means we are not pushing ourselves hard enough; get knocked down seven times, get up eight; it's not what happens to us, but what we do with what happens to us that makes us or breaks us! In every injury, when Dan went through the proper steps of rehab, every body part that was broken, injured, and repaired became stronger and more stable than it had been before the injury and surgery. It really is true—rainbows follow rain!

0 26575 70398 6